Personality Indicators and the Spiritual Life

Robert Innes

Lecturer in Systematic Theology at St John's College, Durham
and Assistant Curate at St Cuthbert's Church, Durham

GROVE BOOKS LIMITED
RIDLEY HALL RD CAMBRIDGE CB3 9HU

Contents

Acknowledgements

I should like to thank the Grove Spirituality Group for their encouragement to me in the production of this booklet. I am particularly grateful to Dr Lawrence Osborn and Revd Graham Pigott for their very helpful comments. I should also like to thank Dr Jocelyn Bryan (Tutor, Wesley Studies Centre, Durham) for reviewing the draft from a psychological perspective.

The Cover Illustration is by Robert Innes

First Impression May 1996
ISSN 0262-799X
ISBN 1 85174 314 6

1
Introduction

I have grown up in an age of personality testing.

- At school, the careers master had an enthusiasm for psychology and gave groups of us personality tests. Catching on quickly to how these things work, and wanting to appear popular, I engineered myself the most extrovert score in our group. Well, what self-respecting schoolboy would want to admit to reading books rather than going to late-night parties?
- When I joined an American firm of business consultants, I discovered that the annual week's training course invariably featured a personality analysis of some kind. The main aim of these tests was to help us to appreciate the different styles of working and the different gifts that our colleagues were endowed with so that we would be better team players. The firm was quick to point out that those who had reached the top represented a balance of the different personality types. 'Whatever your type, our company needs you' was the message.
- When my fiancée and I went for marriage preparation classes the rural vicar turned out to have been a psychologist in a previous life. He suggested Helen and I take part in a psychological test, not to determine if we were suitable for each other, but so that we might be better equipped to deal with any potential incompatibilities. Helen's view of me was sufficiently generous that I turned out to have a near-ideal personality, whereas my view of her already contained enough hard-headed realism to reveal one or two dangerous looking spikes in her profile!
- Whilst I have been associated with St John's College, Durham we have introduced, not uncontroversially, a Myers-Briggs workshop for our ordinands. If personality testing can be applied to school, marriage and work, perhaps it can also be applied to relationships in church, and even to the relationship with God that we work out in prayer.

What I should like to do in this booklet is to explore what the value of secular personality indicators might be for furthering our spiritual life. I am going to focus on the two indicators most widely used by Christian groups—Myers Briggs and the Enneagram. Can they help us? Might they harm us? Or are they an irrelevant, if enjoyable, diversion?

2

Journeying in Search of the Self

Before looking at particular personality indicators (perhaps a better word than 'tests') we need to address a fundamental issue. What bearing has knowledge of our own personality on our walk with God? How far is concern for and knowledge of the 'self' a part of the Christian spiritual life? A helpful way into this subject is to look at the roots of our contemporary preference for self-examination. By understanding where our predilection for analysing our personalities comes from, we shall be better placed to understand how far it can contribute to the Christian life. For, as we shall see, a concern with self-knowledge arises from a mixture of Christian and secular sources.

Our Modern Sense of Inwardness

Our modern Western identity is characterized by a sense of 'inwardness.' We conceive ourselves as a complex of states and emotions that lie 'within' ourselves. We have the sense that the further inwards we go the closer we get to the 'real me.' We may well regard ourselves as having a dark and mysterious unconscious that influences how we behave and that is inaccessible even to our own conscious mind. Perhaps surprisingly, anthropologists tell us that this sense of 'inwardness' is quite specific to the modern West.[1] (Compare the ancient Hebrews for whom aspects of what we would call the 'self' were identified with parts of the body such as the heart, lungs and kidneys.) But once we believe, as we now inevitably do, that the 'real me' lies within, we may well want to discover and make explicit this mysterious inner self through indicators and tests of various kinds.

There are a number of cultural and intellectual streams that go to make up our modern 'inward' sense of self.[2] I want to discuss two of the most important. The first stems largely from St Augustine of Hippo and represents the dominant source of Western understandings of the spiritual journey. The second originates with more modern writers such as Montaigne and Rousseau, and in our century Carl Jung. It charts a naturalistic journey inwards and is the main cultural source of some of the personality indicators in use today.

2.1 The Spiritual Journey Inwards

The initiation of the tradition of the Western 'inward' self may be attributed largely to St Augustine. Augustine synthesized the Judaeo-Christian faith and Neo-Platonic philosophy in a way that resulted in a tradition of thought bearing a remarkably inward notion of selfhood. Indeed our modern 'psychological' sense

---

1   See, for example, M Carrithers, S Collins and S Lukes (eds), *The Category of the Person* (CUP, 1985).
2   See further the monumental analysis of this question in Charles Taylor, *Sources of the Self: The Making of the Modern Identity* (CUP, 1992).

of selfhood finds its ultimate ancestor in Augustine. This is not to say that other philosophers such as Plotinus or theologians such as Gregory of Nyssa contemporary with Augustine did not use the language of inwardness. The patristic theologians and desert fathers had the sense of a spiritual interiorism born out of the pursuit of the soul towards the vision of God. Neo-Platonic philosophy operated with a metaphysic in which, through contemplation, human beings might recognize the divine in themselves and restore it to unity with the transcendent source of all being. But Augustine personalized the Neo-Platonic philosophy in the light of his own experiences and Christian religious convictions to a remarkable degree. He has had a far greater effect on the intellectual tradition than his contemporaries.

Augustine held that the search for God requires a turning inward upon oneself. Where Plato's Ideas were to be seen in the field of objects, insofar as these participated in the realm of Ideas, Augustine's God is known in the power of seeing itself. This involves what we might call a 'radically reflexive' stance.[3] God is made known in our experiencing of ourselves. The mind's true self-presence to itself, or what Augustine calls the mind's remembering of itself, must therefore emerge into the mind's remembering of God. For Augustine the inner presence of God is a fundamental theological and philosophical principle, and interiority is therefore a notion that occurs widely in Augustine's writings.

The psychological models of the second half of *de Trinitate* offer some profound examples of Augustine's interiorism. Perhaps most importantly, Augustine's *Confessions* are the first autobiography in the ancient world written with the purpose of describing oneself, one's own character and one's inner life. This book alone marks a major contribution to the modern notion of the self as a person with definite character, complexities, motives and aims.[4]

In the medieval period, patterns of 'inwardness' were sustained especially in the monastic movement. In twelfth century monasticism it appears that the interior way came to predominate over the sense of belonging to the wider body of believers in finding one's path towards God. The writings of authors such as Bernard of Clairvaux, William of St Thierry and Aelred of Rievaulx are marked by a radically reflexive stance in which self-knowledge is seen as fundamental for spiritual growth. Thus Bernard writes: 'Begin by considering yourself—no, rather, end by that...For you, you are the first; you are also the last.'[5] And Aelred exclaims: 'How much does a man know if he does not know himself?'[6] The twelfth century also witnessed a desire for self-expression, as evidenced in a huge increase in the preaching and preservation of sermons, and a flourishing of poetry in which personal emotions and experience were described. Guibert of Nogent

---

3   A term I owe to Charles Taylor.
4   With the Augustinian scholars Peter Brown and Gerald Bonner. See, for example, Prof Bonner's 'Starting With Oneself' *Expository Times*, March 1990, Vol 101, No 6, p 163. *Pace* those who take the *Confessions* to be a meditation on the soul's Neo-Platonic ascent to God.
5   Quoted in Colin Morris, *The Discovery of the Individual 1050-1200* (SPCK Camelot, 1972) p 66.
6   *op cit.*

suggested that the promotion of self-understanding was the main function of the preacher, and that this had to come from the preacher's own self-analysis.[7]

The medieval desire for self-knowledge generated a keen interest in psychology. The starting point here was the work of Augustine. Augustine's psychological trinities fitted well with the monastic concern to find through self-knowledge the way to God. But within the broad lines of Augustine's spiritual psychology, authors such as William of St Thierry (*The Nature and Dignity of Love*, c1120) and Aelred of Rievaulx (*The Mirror of Charity*, c1142) developed a 'clinical theology' of the affections and dispositions which motivate the soul's progress towards God.

The Protestant Reformation signalled a breaking back from medieval theology to the fathers. But in its dependence on Augustine the close linkage between knowledge of God and knowledge of oneself was maintained. Calvin, for example, opens his *Institutes* with the words: 'Without knowledge of self there is no knowledge of God.' Calvin argues that, on the one hand, without examining our own sinfulness we would not become aware of our need for God. However, on the other hand, without a knowledge of God we cannot properly know ourselves. Only in the light of God's standards will we have a proper estimate of our own value and not fall prey to self-deception.

Of course there is much more to say, but I hope that this brief survey has indicated that there is a deep concern for self-knowledge within the Christian spiritual tradition which stems largely from Augustine and which extends to Protestant as well as Catholic theology. An increasing knowledge of ourselves has been seen to be a good and beneficial thing in our growing knowledge of God. Conversely a knowledge of God results in a more accurate and perceptive knowledge of ourselves. A heightened personal awareness is expected to yield a greater openness to God and, hopefully, to the outside world. The spiritual journey into the self leads to a transcendence of self.

2.2 The Natural Journey Inwards

There is a second kind of journey inward that is radically different from that initiated by Augustine. An early exemplar of this search is the sixteenth century French essayist Michel Montaigne. Montaigne goes inward not so much to find God as to discover himself: 'The world always looks outward, I turn my gaze inward, there I fix it, and there I keep it busy. Everyone looks before him; I look within.'[8] Through engaging with his own uniqueness and particularity it seems that Montaigne felt he could, in the face of self-depreciating moral demands to the contrary, learn self-acceptance. 'I have no business but with myself, I unceas-

---

7 Guibert: 'No preaching seems to me more profitable than that which reveals a man to himself...Whoever has the duty of teaching, if he wishes to be perfectly equipped, can first learn in himself, and afterwards profitably teach to others, what the experience of his inner struggles has taught.' (Quoted in Morris, p 67).

8 *Essais* II.17.

ingly consider, examine and analyse myself.'[9]

For Montaigne, the only safe way of establishing a pattern of life was by means of knowledge of one's own self.[10] Where Augustine understood the self as the rational, spiritual self, Montaigne saw it as the natural self. 'I have…quite simply and crudely accepted for my own use the ancient rule that we cannot go wrong in following nature, and that the sovereign precept is to conform to her…I let myself go on as I come; I struggle against nothing; my two dominant parts live, of their own accord in peace and amity.'[11] Montaigne's advice is one of the first precursors of the discovery and acceptance of opposing parts of the self, recommended in our century by Carl Jung.[12]

Another Frenchman, Jean-Jacques Rousseau, offered a statement of the 'natural self' which has been particularly influential in modern psychological notions of self-exploration. Rousseau's *Confessions* share many similarities with Augustine's book of the same name, not least an intense exposition of the subject's sexuality. But Rousseau marked a fundamental objection to the Augustinian theological tradition by his rejection of Augustine's doctrine of original sin in favour of his own notion of natural goodness: 'Let us set down as an incontestable maxim that the first movements of nature are always right. There is no original perversity in the human heart.'[13] Where Augustine turned inward in recognition of his inadequacy and dependence on God, Rousseau's inward turn hoped to make contact with the innate goodness of the human soul.

Whilst most Christians would not go along fully with Rousseau, his emphasis on natural goodness has proved for many to be a helpful counter to the pessimistic view of the fallen self expressed by Augustine. An overemphasis on our fallenness has sometimes led both Catholics and Evangelicals towards self-punishing or self-hating forms of spirituality. There is surely goodness as well as sin in the human soul. Contemporary theologians have tried to respond to this conviction by recovering alternative patristic notions of creation and fall, notably that of Irenaeus, who sees the fall more as an interruption of the process of human growth rather than as the catastrophic obliteration of the divine image envisaged by Augustine.

Rousseau identifies goodness with self-responsible freedom. Rousseau's ideal man, 'Emile,' is someone who can find reasons for action from within himself, who acts autonomously. He is capable of relationships of deep friendship and love, and he feels a general sense of benevolence towards humanity, but he does

---

9 op cit.
10 So John Holyoake, *Contextual and Thematic Inferences in Montaigne's Essais* (Sheffield: Sheffield Academic Press, 1986).
11 *Essais* III.12.
12 Jung liked to trace the roots of his ideas through medieval alchemy back to Gnosticism. However, where the Gnostics rejected the natural in favour of the spiritual, Jung signals a distinctively modern commitment to the natural self. His emphasis on the discovery and acceptance of the natural realm lying within the psyche places him in the modern current of thought I outline here.
13 Jean-Jacques Rousseau, *Emile* (Penguin, 1991) p 92.

not fall into unhealthy relationships of dominance and dependence.

Rousseau's quest for autonomy through regaining contact with the natural, inner self has been taken up in our century by those many popular psychologists who advocate 'self-help.' 'If only I were properly in touch with myself I would know how to act,' is the general theme. Once we start thinking about ourselves in these terms then any personality test or indicator that promises to reveal our inner self (or deepest preferences) becomes very interesting. Indeed understanding our own selves becomes a moral imperative: if it is from within myself rather than from an authoritative text or from other people that I discover meaning then I have a moral duty to discover as much about myself as possible.

In our own century the quest for the 'natural self' has been taken up by two schools of psychology in particular.

1. Carl Jung thought that the human psyche is composed of numerous parts including the surface, conscious 'persona' that we show to the world, and a hidden, 'shadow' that we hide from the world and indeed from ourselves. In order to grow psychologically Jung thought we need to learn about and accept our own shadow. The conclusion of this process of self-discovery and self-acceptance is the emergence from our unconscious depths of our real identity, something that Jung calls the archetype of the 'Self.' Jung's 'Self' is closely related to what he calls 'God;' indeed Jung is reluctant to speak about a God who might exist independently of the Self. Whereas in the Christian tradition learning about oneself is a means to the greater goal of knowing God, in Jung's psychology discovering one's Self is an end in itself.

   Carl Jung's psychology lies behind one of the most popular of the personality indicators used by Christian groups, the Myers-Briggs Type Indicator.

2. The broad area known as humanistic psychology has taken up the quest for the natural self in a rather different way. Humanistic psychology derives in part from the work of a group of so-called 'personality theorists' in the 1930s who included among their number Goldstein, Allport and (most famously) Abraham Maslow. These people were interested in developing forms of psychology that took seriously the wholeness and uniqueness of the person. Their ideas eventually led to the formation in 1962 of the American Association for Humanistic Psychology. Humanistic psychology emphasizes the natural goodness and worth of the human person and is concerned to develop human potential through warm supportive relationships. Carl Rogers' counselling theory is one of the most influential applications of humanistic psychology. Humanistic ideas were disseminated and popularized most especially through the Esalen Institute founded at Big Sur, California in 1962. Esalen effectively functions as a clearing house for all kinds of humanistic and 'New Age' self-help techniques and therapies.

   The second of the personality indicators widely used by Christian groups, the Enneagram, was first 'marketed' and made available to a Western audience by Esalen, notably through the efforts of Claudio Naranjo.

3

The Origins of the
Two Most Popular Type Indicators

3.1 The Myers Briggs Type Indicator

The Myers Briggs Type Indicator (MBTI®) was developed by Katherine Briggs and her daughter, whose married name was Isabel Briggs Myers. Mrs Briggs senior became fascinated by the similarities and differences between people, and around the time of the first World War began to develop her own typology of personality. She then discovered that the psychologist Carl Jung had developed a similar system which she quickly accepted and began to explore and elaborate. Isabel shared her mother's enthusiasm for Jung's theory of types, and she continued to work with her mother on a means of measuring and quantifying Type. The initial application of the Indicator was intended to be that of helping to place people in jobs that would match their personality preferences. In 1971 a 'typology laboratory' was created in Florida to develop a data bank for research, and in 1975 the MBTI® questionnaire was published in a widely accessible form. In 1980 Isabel Myers published her book 'Gifts Differing' which explains the development and use of the type indicator. The MBTI® was subsequently taken over by Consulting Psychologists Press, Inc of Palo Alto California who now market the indicator.[14]

Jung's primary distinction was between extrovert and introvert types. He suggested extroversion (E) derives from the direction of a person's energy (or what Jung calls 'libido') outwards towards others, whereas introversion (I) results from the direction of energy inwards towards the self. Jung's insight that we can distinguish traits of extroversion and introversion has been widely and generally accepted.[15] It accords with our common sense experience that some people are bubbly and outgoing whilst others tend to be quiet and reserved. Some like to be surrounded by people, others prefer the company of a few close friends. Indeed the strictly empirical psychologist Hans Eysenck, who would in other respects not at all be associated with Jung, has used an extroversion/introversion score as one of the bases of his own personality indicator.[16]

---

14 Note that MBTI is a trademark and Myers-Briggs Type Indicator is a registered trademark of Consulting Psychologists Inc. The administration of MBTI® is restricted to accredited practitioners. However, many people have become aware of the Myers-Briggs typology through the modification to the system put forward by David Kiersey (David Kiersey and Marilyn Bates, *Please Understand Me* (Del Mar, Prometheus Nemesis Books, 1978)). Kiersey's modified version works with pairs of types; its use is not protected in the same way as MBTI®, and it therefore tends to be more widely available.

15 Although Christians would not allow this classification the *determinative* influence on one's psychology and spirituality that Jung claimed for it.

16 The Eysenck Personality Questionnaire (EPQ) whose other bases are neuroticism and psychoticism.

Going beyond the basic E/I attitudes, Jung identified the four primary psychological 'functions' of thinking (T), feeling (F), sensation (S) and intuition (N). 'Thinking' and 'Feeling' he termed 'rational' or 'judging' functions since they are complementary ways of arriving at a reasoned decision.[17] 'Thinking' approaches decision making by way of objective criteria such as truth/falsity. 'Feeling' is Jung's somewhat vague term used to encompass all other ways of making decisions, including judgments of value (good/bad) and aesthetic taste. Sensation and Intuition, on the other hand, were to be conceived of as non-rational, or pre-rational, functions that deal with the immediate apprehension of data.

Based on a study of historical figures and through observing his own patients, Jung hypothesized that people tend to develop one dominant rational and one non-rational function in addition to their basic E/I attitude. By combining one each of E/I, T/F and S/N we arrive at eight possible permutations of psychological types.

However, Jung's further subdivisions of feeling, thinking, sensation and intuition are problematic. It is not at all clear that T/F and S/I functions are really as distinct as Jung tries to argue. In practice we do not usually evaluate an entity's goodness or badness (F function) completely independently from evaluating its truthfulness or falsity (T function). Even so 'T' an activity as pure mathematics has quite a well developed component of F-type sensitivity to aesthetic beauty. On the other hand, even so 'F' an activity as writing poetry requires a high level of 'thinking' for the production of well-crafted verse. Again, in order to have a well-developed 'intuition' we actually need to be particularly sensitive to sensory stimuli. On the other hand no one will develop a very highly developed discrimination of externally perceived objects (S) without some conceptual framework within which to organize the data (N).

It is considerations like these that led the psychologist Anthony Storr (who is basically sympathetic to Jung) to comment that 'this further classification of types is one of Jung's least satisfactory contributions.'[18] In Storr's judgment Jung's quaternity of four functions 'has been discarded by all except the most dedicated Jungians, and is little used even by them.'[19] The community of Myers Briggs users would appear to be an important exception to Storr's rule! To be fair to Jung, I do not think that he expected or even especially welcomed the great interest that has been shown in his theory of eight types. In the foreword to a later edition of his work on psychological types he suggested that he had merely offered the types as a means of organizing the empirical material, and he warned those who sought to 'type' people that 'this kind of classification is nothing but a childish parlour game.'[20]

Mrs Myers and Mrs Briggs offered a further refinement to the Jungian theory

17 *CW* 6, pp 359ff and 391ff; and see the discussion in Anthony Stevens, *On Jung* (Penguin, 1991) p 196f.
18 Anthony Storr, *Jung* (Fontana, 1986) p 77.
19 Storr, p 79.
20 *CW* 6, p xiv.

of eight types by introducing a distinction between judging (J) and perceiving (P) types and now allowing for sixteen possible types overall. According to Consulting Psychologists Press Inc, if you are a 'J' (Judging) type 'you like a planned and organized approach to life and prefer to have things settled.' By contrast, if you are a 'P' (Perceiving) type 'you like a flexible and spontaneous approach to life and prefer to keep your options open.' Their contrast between order and spontaneity can, I think, be overplayed. One ought to order one's life so as to cultivate desirable forms of spontaneity (such as unhesitating generosity) and so as to eliminate undesirable forms (such as an explosive temper). However, as we observe our fellow human-beings it seems broadly reasonable to suppose that some are more at home with, or have a preference for, spontaneity, whilst others have a preference for planning.

In academic psychological terms there are important questions to be raised about what is termed the 'validity' of the MBTI®. Does it actually measure what it claims to measure? Can one really move from the limited set of questions given in the MBTI® questionnaire to the very general descriptions of personality type offered by Consulting Psychologists Inc? It may be that what the MBTI® instrument actually measures is a much narrower set of psychological attributes than what is claimed.[21]

Having said this, my experience is that those people who take the MBTI® do broadly recognize themselves in the type descriptions offered. In other words, it seems that despite some serious theoretical questions over the classification employed the indicator has practical value. Indeed I well remember the experience of the former principal of my theological college who, despite being armed with numerous theoretical objections to MBTI® discovered to his surprise that, at least so far as his own family was concerned, it worked!

This is, perhaps, not as surprising as it appears on first sight. It seems perfectly possible that, given enough empirical work, one could devise a set of questions and a set of type descriptions such that those who complete the questionnaire usually recognize themselves in the associated type descriptions. The art of writing the type descriptions is presumably to make them sufficiently general that one includes as many people as possible but sufficiently specific that respondents feel they are reading more than their horoscope.

MBTI® succeeds, in so far as it does succeed, by giving people a language in which they can interpret themselves and describe themselves to others. MBTI®'s language functions both to affirm the individual (it's OK to be an 'I' after all!) and to help us be sensitive to differences in others (I can see that because she is an 'E' she has a different temperament and different needs from me). Its limitations

---

21 See, for example, Paul Kline, *Personality: the Psychometric View* (Routledge, 1993). The question of the 'validity' of MBTI® opens out into the question of the 'validity' of psychometric testing in general—a technical (though important) issue which goes beyond the scope of this booklet. Questions of validity are of crucial importance if one intends using psychological tests to assess candidates suitability for employment, as is currently being proposed by the Church of England's Advisory Board of Ministry.

arise from the inevitable restrictions that classification under sixteen types places people who are as phenomenally diverse as human beings. You and I literally defy classification; we will invariably find something of the 'opposite' type in ourselves and find that the Myers-Briggs 'type' does not wholly fit the 'real me.' If one thinks too hard about the theoretical basis of MBTI® one runs into problems, but used in a suitably non-dogmatic way it can be enlightening and of some value.

3.2 The Enneagram

The Enneagram is a circle with nine points on it (from Greek *ennea* meaning nine and *gram* meaning line drawing). Inside the circle two figures connect the nine points: a triangle and an oddly-shaped six pointed entity. The overall visual effect is roughly that of a nine-pointed star inscribed in a circle. This unusual diagram (see front cover) forms the basis of a personality typology which is itself known as 'the Enneagram' and which has been used by numbers of American Jesuits and through them by Roman Catholics in America and in Europe.

Proponents of the Enneagram are fond of saying that its origins are shrouded in mystery, which indeed they are. The best account of its genesis of which I am aware is that given by Mitchell Pacwa SJ, Professor of Scripture and Hebrew at Loyola University, Chicago, and which I shall follow closely.[22]

The man credited with bringing the Enneagram to the West is George Gurdjieff, a Greek-Armenian from what is now the Republic of Georgia. As a teenager Gurdjieff developed a fascination with occultic practices such as astrology, mental telepathy, spiritism, table turning, fortune telling and demon possession. In order to learn more about these occult sciences he travelled widely through Asia and the Near East. The story goes that while he was in Afghanistan, in about 1897, a Sufi mystic introduced him to a monastery of the esoteric Sarmouni sect where he learned their mystical dancing, psychic powers and the Enneagram.

In fact, there is no hard evidence for the existence of the Enneagram in any form before Gurdjieff. Pacwa comments that in his studies of ancient literature and archaeology he has found no evidence of the Enneagram's existence in ancient times, neither inscriptions nor drawings. Rumours of the Enneagram's antiquity serve to give it an air of authority but have no proper historical basis.[23]

After several years of travel in the east, Gurdjieff opened his 'Institute for the Harmonious Development of Man' in Moscow in 1912, an institute which eventually relocated to Paris. Gurdjieff taught that everyone has three personal centres: the mental, located in the head; the emotional, located in the heart; and the physical, located in the belly (beliefs which continue in recent 'Enneagram spir-

---

22 Mitchell Pacwa SJ 'Tell Me Who I Am, O Enneagram' *Christian Research Journal*, Fall 1991, pp 14ff. I am indebted to Dr Lawrence Osborn for supplying me with a copy of this article.

23 Thus I am not aware of any solid evidence to support the suggestion (Maria Beesing, Robert Nogosek and Patrick O'Leary, *The Enneagram: A Journey of Self-Discovery* (Denville: Dimension Books, 1984) p 1) that the Enneagram originated in the early years of pre-Muslim Christian influence of Persia; nor the suggestion (D R Riso, *Personality Types: Using the Enneagram for Self-Discovery* (Aquarian Press, 1987) p 12) that it arises from Pythagorean or Neo-Platonic mathematics.

ituality'). Gurdjieff taught various spiritual exercises which were designed to restore harmony and balance between these three centres. Gurdjieff also taught that everyone has an essence and a personality. The essence is the material of which the universe is made whilst the personality is a mask of compulsive behaviour which covers this essence. Personal growth consists in recognizing and shaking off this compulsive personality so as to return to the essence.

The Enneagram featured prominently in Gurdjieff's teaching and in the writing of his followers. They were particularly interested in the numerological properties of the Enneagram. Dividing one by three yields the decimals .3333, .6666, .9999—the points joined by the triangle in the figure. Dividing one by seven yields the decimal .142857: a recurring number which contains no multiples of three and the digits of which correspond to the oddly-shaped six pointed figure. It seems that the Enneagram's relation to these mystical numbers (three and seven) was held to give it a truly cosmic significance. John Bennett, a Gurdjieff student, commented that the 'Enneagram is more than a picture of yourself, it is yourself…the Enneagram is a living diagram…and we can experience ourselves as Enneagrams.'[24] Indeed, one reason for doubting the Enneagram's antiquity is that it fits so conveniently with the Gurdjieff school's numerologically-inspired view of the world.

Gurdjieff's work led to the formation of many different personal development and training groups, the most influential of which proved to be the 'Arica' training programme founded by Oscar Ichazo. It was Ichazo and his disciple Claudio Naranjo (an instructor at the Esalen Institute) who together developed the Enneagram in the 1960s as an indicator of personality in its current form. Ichazo, like Gurdjieff, has been, it appears, strongly influenced by various eastern and occultic religious practices; Ichazo was familiar with the strange Enneagram figure and wrote personality descriptions for each of the nine points. Naranjo contributed to the personality descriptions and correlated the nine personality compulsions with the Freudian psychological mechanisms of defence.[25] Ichazo and Naranjo taught the Enneagram in the early 1970s to Esalen students including Helen Palmer, author of one of the classic texts on the subject, and to Fr Bob Ochs SJ who then taught it at the Loyola seminary and introduced it to the Catholic community.

The Enneagram's shrouded, mystical origins and strange history of development make it quite different from the kind of scientifically founded and validated personality indicator that an academic psychologist might use. It is better understood as a 'tradition' of thought about the self and the personality. As such, it has been developed and used in a wide variety of ways. As far as I am aware, there is no 'standard' test or methodology for using the Enneagram. One practitioner rightly comments: 'The Enneagram is an oral tradition. Because this is so it is

---

24 John Bennett, *Enneagram Studies* (York Beach, Maine: Samuel Weiser, 1983) p 32, quoted by Pacwa.
25 Although the fact that Anna Freud had developed ten 'mechanisms of defence' not nine seems to be quietly overlooked.

difficult to pinpoint individuals who originated specific reflections on the theory.'[26]

The practitioners do seem to agree on the importance of nine types, on the 'compulsive' nature of each type, and on the need to remedy the compulsion by achieving some kind of psychological balance. However, the descriptions of the nine types and their relation to the three centres of mind, heart and belly seem to be quite flexible. Thus one system of classification talks of the primacy of the three faculties of feeling, doing and relating and suggests that the nine compulsions arise from unbalanced combinations of these three.[27] Another group of authors speak of compulsions as tending to move us along one of the lines of the Enneagram and of redemption as a counterbalancing move backwards along the lines.[28] A third author places the whole of the Enneagram within a basically Jungian framework and suggests that our task is to become aware of the parts of the personality which tend to be underdeveloped.[29]

From the perspectives of both theology and psychology there appear to be some large question marks over this particular personality indicator.

- Why should we believe that there are 'nine, and only nine, types of human personality'?[30] Why not sixteen (the Myers-Briggs answer), or 42 (the answer at the end of the universe)? What real authority does this kind of division, which possesses no proper empirical validation, and the origins of whose theory are hazy to say the least, really possess? From a Christian point of view (or indeed from a scientific point of view) it is obviously not adequate to argue that the nine types reflect the nine colours of the rainbow or that it is consonant with Sufi ideas about the nine manifestations of the Divine.[31]
- The Enneagram is rooted in a numerological world-view that is not consistent with the Christian faith. I do not doubt that many of those who now teach the Enneagram have tried to separate the Enneagram as a psychological tool from the broader philosophy in which it is embedded. Nonetheless, by choosing to use the Enneagram one is subscribing to a way of viewing the self whose primary roots lie in an esoteric outlook far removed from both the Christian faith and scientific rationality.

26 Suzanne Zuercher, *Enneagram Spirituality* (Notre Dame: Ave Maria Press, 1992) p 157.
27 Riso, *op cit.*
28 Beesing *et al, op cit.*
29 Zuercher.
30 Beesing *et al*, p 5.
31 Zuercher, p 8.

4

The Question of Personality and Personality Indicators

The notion of 'personality' is extraordinarily difficult to define. Like many words, it is perhaps best understood not in the abstract but by seeing what it means in the various psychological theories in which it is used. It might therefore be helpful to set out some of the most influential psychological schools of thought on the personality so as to outline how each uses the term.[32]

- Type theories assume that the personality is a function of physiological type. Thus the ancient Greek philosopher Galen supposed that our temperament was determined by the mixture of four body fluids and that our temperament type (sanguine, melancholic, choleric or phlegmatic) depended on which of the fluids was dominant. In recent psychology, W H Sheldon argued that our personality is dependent on body types. Carl Jung's approach does not relate personality type to physiology in this way and, whilst it is often discussed as a 'type' theory, and will be here, it is in some respects better described within the category of psychodynamic theories (see below).[33]
- Trait theories assume that one's personality is made up of a composite of 'traits' or characteristic ways of behaving. Thus R B Cattell thought that there are a set of 'source traits' which exist in everyone in varying quantities and which are the determinants of personality. Where 'type' approaches focus on what is common amongst different personalities, 'trait' approaches focus on what makes individuals different.
- Psychodynamic theories stress the wholeness and integration of the personality, and they pay attention to the influence of developmental factors on personality. Each of them suggests some underlying motivational force for personality growth. Thus Freud talks of the importance of the sex-drive, Jung's psychology is based on the drive to individuation, and Maslow's theory assumes a drive towards self-actualization.

  Whilst MBTI® is one stage removed from its underlying Jungian psychology, in view of its basic independence from physiological explanations of temperament it is strictly better classed as a 'psychodynamic' theory than as a 'type' theory.[34]
- Behaviourism and Social learning theories focus on the influence of the environment and on what has been learnt through rewards and punishments (rather

---

32 Ref. Arthur Reber, *Dictionary of Psychology* (Penguin, 1985).
33 Note in this regard David Kiersey's attempt to correlate his pairs of Myers-Briggs types with Galen's temperaments: SP (sanguine), SJ (melancholic), NT (phlegmatic) and NF (choleric).
34 So Kline, p 136.

than on what has been inherited as a type or trait) as determinants of personality.

* Situationism, advocated by Walter Mischel, argues that whatever consistency of behaviour is observable is largely determined by the characteristics of the situation rather than by any internal personality or traits. Indeed, the very notion of a personality is, on this view, merely a construct in the mind of the observer who uses it to try to make sense of the behaviour of others. The regularity of behaviour is attributed to the similarity of the situations one observes another in, rather than to an underlying internal personality.

As a theologian I would want to draw on the insights of all the approaches. However, the variety among them at least causes me to be cautious about putting too many eggs in any one basket. I must be reluctant, therefore, to assume that a particular approach, let us say a variety of the 'type' approach to personality, has all the answers. A type theory may be helpful on some occasions but it may be unhelpful on others.

Let me give an example. A friend of mine turns up half an hour late for a social engagement. What kind of explanation might I give? I could put it down to my friend being a strong Myers-Briggs 'P' type—spontaneous rather than organized. Alternatively, I might put it down to the trait he occasionally shows of being a touch inconsiderate. Then again, I might inquire as to whether he has learnt to be late—he knows I do not get upset if he doesn't keep to appointments. Or, there may be cultural factors involved: he might use his lateness as a social cue to indicate his superiority in status to me. Finally, it might be that there was something in this particular situation which made him late—the baby sitter was delayed. All of these, or none of them, might help me with an explanation. But, by itself, knowing my friend's Myers-Briggs type may be no help at all. It could even be worse than useless if it encourages me to put his behaviour down to his 'type' when there is some other more urgent reason at stake.

This kind of reasoning throws some light on the (limited) value of 'type' theories for the spiritual life. I discover that a member of my youth club seldom prays. What am I to make of this behaviour? Knowing him to be a Myers-Briggs ESTJ I could take it that his type do not have a natural inclination towards prayer but prefer to spend their time playing football with their mates. Alternatively, I could put it down to a trait he has for being a little lazy about things which require concentration. Or is it that he has not been brought up and taught to pray? Finally, it could be that he has organized his life in such a way that there is never a time to pray—the situation is never right. Here again a knowledge of 'types' may or may not be of use.

As a Christian and a theologian I am not, however, willing to leave it entirely to the psychologists to tell me about human personality. For as a Christian I believe that human beings are motivated quite decisively by one thing which none of the psychologists have mentioned, namely the desire for God. In a quite fundamental sense our spiritual health or sickness is worked out according as whether our desire for God is realized or frustrated. We are now in the arena of divine grace and human faith, of our weakness being met by divine strengthening, of our sin being healed by his forgiveness. It is these realities which are of the essence of the spiritual life. The primary consideration for my non-praying youth club member is whether or not he knows himself as a forgiven sinner and therefore wants to pray as a means of growing in his relationship with God. If, deep down, he really wants to pray then we can find ways round and through the other issues. Psychological analysis may have a secondary value in, for example, highlighting false images of God and of prayer, or in dealing with resistances to prayer, such as fear or inappropriate self-judgment.

We need, too, to be aware of some of the practical difficulties involved in obtaining meaningful results from the personality indicators. The MBTI®, like many other indicators, is of the 'self-report' kind. This means the indicator tells you only what you have first told it; there is no assessment or correction of your responses by some third party. Self-report indicators can only be of value if your view of your self is accurately reflected in your reported answers, in the jargon if your self-report accurately reflects your self-concept. The psychologist R B Burns has suggested six factors which can cause a divergence between the two:[35]

a) The clarity of the individual's self-awareness
b) The availability of adequate symbols for expression
c) The willingness of the individual to cooperate
d) Social expectancy
e) The individual's feelings of personal adequacy
f) The individual's feelings of freedom from threat.

In practice it may be rather difficult to attain a high level of 'truth-telling.' We very easily deceive ourselves either consciously or unconsciously. Some tests have 'lie-detectors' built in so that the administrator's suspicions are alerted if the respondent appears to be giving answers in accordance with expectations rather than in line with his or her self-concept.[36] The MBTI® attempt to address this problem involves encouraging speed of response to the questions posed. This may, perhaps, eliminate at least the grosser forms of premeditated deception but does not constitute a solution.

Importantly, the indicator measures your own report about yourself: this may or may not accord with how others see you. I may accurately report my image of myself as a caring, people-centred man, but my wife may equally well see me as someone who prefers to absent himself from his family in favour of his computer screen.

---

35 R B Burns, *The Self Concept in Theory, Measurement, Development and Behaviour* (Longman, 1979) p 75.
36 For example, the EPQ.

5
The Value of Personality Indicators for the Spiritual Life

5.1 Benefits

1. Growth in Self-Knowledge

Self-knowledge is closely related to knowledge of God: the better we understand ourselves the more opportunities we give to our spiritual life to flourish. Indeed all genuine growth in self-knowledge is a good thing. Personality indicators can help us to understand ourselves better and insofar as they do this they are to be welcomed.

2. Appropriate Growth in Self-Love

Those indicators inspired by a Jungian psychology have, as an implicit agenda, the fostering of self-love. One of the central tenets of Jung's psychology was that we need to learn to love and accept the whole of ourselves. Following Jung, the Myers-Briggs type descriptions, for example, are all written in very positive language. They carry the underlying sub-text that you are acceptable and worthy whatever your personality.

Perhaps the major neurosis of our age is lack of self-esteem and self-acceptance. Christian theology, especially in its Protestant forms, has been unenthusiastic about the merits of self-love. Yet an appropriate love of ourselves as God's created beings is surely to be encouraged. Frequently it is only as we properly love ourselves that we can begin to address areas of pain and sin in our lives. Therefore insofar as an exploration of our own personality fosters an appropriate love and acceptance of our God-given nature it is to be encouraged.

3. Enhanced Sensitivity to Others

Many people have found that the most valuable aspect of taking a personality indicator is that it has helped them to clarify their relationship with significant others, perhaps a spouse or a group of colleagues. The personality indicator offers a grammar which can crystallize differences of approach and attitude which people have always sensed were there but no-one has yet put into words. For those with only rudimentary powers of sensitivity to others, a personality indicator can have an almost revelatory impact on their understanding of another.

At a more 'political' level a group of colleagues who know each other well can use a personality indicator to provide a neutral language with which profound differences between them can be safely opened-up and discussed. This use seems to be particularly suited to Anglican clergy groups, for we have a particular cultural penchant for talking about things obliquely and in code. I myself have watched as colleagues have discussed awkward differences quite safely and humorously under the guise of a Myers-Briggs code.

I am aware of one theological college where a Myers-Briggs workshop functions to increase the sensitivity and tolerance of ordinands to those coming from different traditions and with different viewpoints. If a particular outlook or prayer-style can be seen to be a reflection of someone's personality then it gains a certain degree of legitimacy. 'You're different from me, but now I see that it's OK that we are different.' It is, perhaps, unfortunate that Christians can't learn mutual tolerance and respect through more direct means. However, in the intense atmosphere of a theological college a personality test can provide an alternative vocabulary to that of more highly-charged theological terms and symbols for the expression and recognition of differences.

4. Enabling Awareness of Alternative Ways of Praying

Many people have found that a personality indicator opens up for them new forms of praying. The indicators have been one of the ways in recent years in which Christians have been made aware of traditions of praying other than the one in which they had been brought up. This has been particularly important for Evangelicals, for whom a 'prayer and personality' workshop may be a way into imaginative kinds of prayer beyond the sometimes narrowly focused Bible and word-centred forms that Evangelical spirituality has traditionally sanctioned.

Several spiritual authors have attempted to link forms of prayer directly with particular aspects of the personality. Thus Michael and Norrisey, have suggested that particular temperaments have a preference for particular forms of prayer.[37] They argue that 'SJ' types benefit from Ignatian prayer, 'NF' types from what they call 'Augustinian' prayer, 'SP' types from 'Franciscan' prayer and 'NT' types from 'Thomistic' prayer.

This kind of correlation is beset with problems. I am not sure that St Francis would have recognized himself as a 'Franciscan' prayer, nor Augustine as an 'Augustinian'! And supposing that, as some practitioners suggest, we pray with a mode other than our 'dominant' preference for relating to the world? Despite the large claims made by Michael and Norrisey, a straw poll of the members of the Grove Spirituality Group indicated that none of us had actually found their specific recommendations of prayer methods for our 'type' helpful. Moreover, it seems likely that any spiritual tradition that has stood the test of time should have sufficient diversity to accommodate people of very different temperaments.[38]

An alternative approach suggested by Bruce Duncan is that the well-rounded prayer life should involve prayers which exercise all the different functions of the personality. Duncan wisely notes that 'people who share the same Myers-Briggs

---

37 Chester Michael and Marie Norrisey, *Prayer and Temperament* (Charlottesville: Open Door Inc, 1984) following Kiersey's modification to Myers-Briggs. See also Charles Keating, *Who We Are is How We Pray* (Mystic 23rd Publications, 1987).

38 See further Lawrence and Diana Osborn, *God's Diverse People* (Darton, Longman & Todd, 1991) ch 4, 'Personalities in Prayer.'

type do not necessarily prefer to pray in the same way.'[39] Duncan suggests that we discover our spiritual 'home-style' of prayer and then go out from there to explore the other kinds and styles of prayer that are around in the Christian tradition.

Like Duncan I am cautious about attempts to link personality type to prayer styles directly. However, personality indicators can be of benefit to our prayer life insofar as they open up to us neglected aspects of our selves and ways of praying of which we were previously unaware. Two particular instances suggest themselves.

First, we may have been socialized into a form of prayer which is no longer appropriate to our stage of personal and spiritual development and which we may need to move on from in order to grow in spiritual maturity. Our prayer must reflect our personal growth more generally.

Secondly, we may benefit from praying in ways that balance the mental functions that we use most intensively in our work. For example, if we most regularly think in abstract, conceptual terms, we may do well to experiment with prayers that involve concrete images and objects. Our prayer may be most recreative when it meets some of our needs for relaxation and uses our less dominant modes of thinking.

The kind of suggestions made by Michael and Norrisey have provided a convenient means of granting permission to many to explore other traditions. The practical impact of their theorizing has been beneficial to many. We must now, however, ask if we should not continue to explore and enjoy a diversity of traditions without needing recourse to this particular (and, it appears, unfounded) alibi.

5. Fun

Let's face it, many of us do personality indicators because they are fun. Most of us enjoy analysing ourselves and talking about ourselves with others. Personality indicators provide an excellent end of term or mid-course activity as a diversion from more serious work. They can, quite reasonably, be understood as a form of play.

5.2 Pitfalls

1. A Narcissistic Focus on the Self

If the dominant neurosis of our age is poor self-esteem perhaps our major besetting sin is narcissism: an excessive self-love or a concern to gain emotional gratification from the contemplation of our own selves. We try to compensate for our poor feelings about ourselves by plunging into ourselves. The seeking of resources from within our own selves has a long cultural history, as I indicated in

---

39 Bruce Duncan, *Pray Your Way: Your Personality and God* (Darton, Longman & Todd, 1993) p 85.

my discussion of the 'Natural Self.' To some extent exploration of our selves helps us grow in understanding of our selves and it can also be fun. Yet carried too far it is disastrous—and for two reasons.

Firstly, in the Christian understanding we learn true self-love through seeing ourselves as God sees us. It is above all the doctrine of justification by grace through faith which guarantees our worthiness. If we really know ourselves to be justified and accepted by God then we will be able to accept ourselves. It is only as we know ourselves loved by God that we are properly able to value and love ourselves. By evaluating and analysing ourselves independently of God and of others we risk simply getting caught in spirals of self-concern.

Secondly, so many of our problems—including our psychological problems—are social in nature.[40] The really big problems facing the world and the church are social ones: learning to live in harmony with the earth; the search for justice between the rich north and the poor south; finding common values for our society; combating the erosion of local communities; building healthy families; the evangelization of the nation. In the face of these problems we do not have the luxury of spending excessive time contemplating our own personalities. For some, the interest in personality indicators may indeed be a valid part of their struggle to relate better in a competitive, fragmented world. But, the church's burgeoning interest in personality indicators may itself be an indicator of a deeper spiritual problem, with the danger of fostering spiritual lives that are turned inwards on ourselves not outwards to the world.

2. A Neglect of the Social Dimensions of Personhood

From Augustine onwards Western spirituality and culture have moved in the direction of giving us a notion of the person as an individual bearer of a set of psychological attributes. However, we need also to listen to voices outside this Western tradition which give us a more social understanding of what it is to be a person. In particular Eastern Orthodoxy offers us a notion of the person which is informed by profound theological reflection on the divine Trinity. This is at least etymologically a good place to start, for the meaning of our word 'person' grew and developed through its use in the early church's debates over the nature of the persons of the Trinity.

Our understanding of the Trinity is that each of the three persons always exists in relation to the other two. We simply cannot picture the Father existing without the Son or the Son without the Father. One of the most important interpreters of Eastern orthodoxy to the West, John Zizioulas, has argued on this basis that personhood is intrinsically relational.[41] In Zizioulas's view the Western notion of the individual is pathological; it indicates a fall out of relationship with God and

---

40 For a strongly argued case that our contemporary neuroses derive from the collapse of community see, for example, Philip Rieff, *The Triumph of the Therapeutic* (New York: Harper and Row, 1968) or, more recently, Christopher Lasch, *The Culture of Narcissism: American Life in an Age of Diminishing Expectations* (Abacus, 1985).

41 John Zizioulas, *Being as Communion* (New York: St Vladimir's Seminary, 1993).

with others. We become true persons only as we are restored to relationship in the community of the church.

Zizioulas's argument, which has carried a great deal of force in theological circles, suggests that we discover ourselves not in isolation from others but precisely through being in relation with others. I know myself not mainly through reflection on myself, or through filling in questionnaires about myself, but through seeing who I am in my relationships. The church, then, offers an alternative way of self-knowledge from the secular personality indicator. It offers (or could offer) a community in which we learn to know ourselves as redeemed persons in fellowship with God and with others.

3. Endowing the Indicators With Too Much Authority

The better books (e.g. Duncan, Palmer) quite properly warn us against assuming that the indicators reveal 'the truth' of the human personality. Nevertheless, when you are actually using one you have to think and talk as if it were true. Once one has been on the relevant workshop, the typology tends to become part of the way we view people. We may now interpret others, quite unconsciously, as if the typology were true.

Whilst, to their credit, the guides do warn against typecasting and pigeon-holing, the very convenience of a set of nine or sixteen labels means this remains a serious risk. Yet it will simply not do to explain or justify behaviour by a naive appeal to type. Stereotyping on grounds of personality type is no more acceptable than it is on any other grounds.

Note that academic psychologists generally grant remarkably little authority to the two indicators I have discussed. The Enneagram is too esoteric to feature in serious scientific discussions, whilst the MBTI® is, at least according to one leading authority, 'of unproven validity.'[42] The indicators provide a popular language with which we may describe ourselves to ourselves and to others, but let us not suppose that they are endowed with either revelatory or scientific power to uncover the truth about ourselves.

4. The Risk of Fostering Misplaced Priorities in Prayer

When one of the disciples asked Jesus 'Lord, teach us to pray' (Luke 11.2), Jesus did not respond by administering a personality test, nor by sending the disciples on a workshop, nor indeed by suggesting any other special techniques. Indeed one of the major differences between the Bible and a guide such as *Zen and the Art of Motor-Cycle Maintenance* is that the latter offers a variety of special techniques whereas the former suggests very little in this direction.

Our culture fosters an interest in technology and techniques. No doubt the

---

42 Paul Kline, *Personality*, p 79. Kline is Professor of psychometrics—the branch of psychology which deals with personality testing—at Exeter university. After reviewing the statistical evidence relating to the Jungian classification, Kline concludes that: 'There has been no clear support for the 8-fold categorization, despite the popularity of the Myers-Briggs Type Indicator' (p 136).

popularity of the personality indicators is in part a response to this culture in the arena of the spiritual life. Yet Jesus's own instruction on prayer is very simple. Pray for your daily needs, for the coming of the kingdom, for forgiveness to be given and received, and for freedom from temptation. It is all very practical and down to earth. The emphasis is on God and his kingdom, not on technique.

Some of the personality-indicator based guides to prayer make large claims for their methods. The impression is given that the personality indicator conveys a kind of esoteric knowledge which, once given, will make prayer easy. We learn of the 'wonderful benefits of self-understanding'[43] conferred by the MBTI® and we are told of the 'new self-understanding and practical guidelines for achieving healing' conferred by the 'amazing insight' of the Enneagram.[44] However, ever since Paul wrote to the Corinthians the Christian tradition has always been wary of claims to amazing insight and knowledge, especially when they come from esoteric (or Gnostic) sources.

The reality is that there are no short cuts to knowledge of God and ourselves. Augustine was absolutely right in picturing the growth in such knowledge as a lifelong pilgrimage in which enlightenment was achieved slowly and often with difficulty. Personality indicators may give us a step on the way but they are no substitute for the steady and sustained growth in spirituality offered by a regular and disciplined prayer-life.

There is a certain quality of *toughness* that characterizes a genuinely Christian spirituality but which can be missing in those kinds of spirituality which focus on the development of our own personality. The turning point in Mark's gospel (Mark 8) is Peter's recognition of the identity of the Christ and Jesus's subsequent revelation to the disciples that their vocation is to be one of self-denial: 'If any man would come after me let him deny himself and take up his cross and follow me.' This is not at all to say that we are to hate ourselves. But, rather, we are to have a certain forgetfulness of self. The gospel message is that we are liberated from self-concern to follow the one whose service is perfect freedom.

I readily accept that self-denial can take many kinds of pathological forms, as the history of our faith and the insights of the modern psychologists make clear.[45] Yet there is a proper denial of self which insists that only if we love God above all else (including ourselves) will our lives be ordered aright.

Finally we need continually to remind ourselves and to treasure the Christian emphasis on the corporate nature of prayer. The Spirit was given when the disciples were praying and worshipping all together in one place (Acts 2.1). Some feel we ought to design our church services so that they appeal to particular personality types. This would seem to me a sad departure from the New Testament notion of the body of Christ. Rather than have my own prayer personality preferences pandered to in church, it is surely better that I sacrifice my 'ideal' way of praying

---

43 Michael and Norrisey, p 8.
44 Beesing *et al*, p 3.
45 See, for example, Anna Freud, *The Ego and the Mechanisms of Defence* (Hogarth Press, 1976) especially ch 10 'A form of altruism.'

in favour of the demand that all of us pray together, notwithstanding that a well-structured act of worship will contain elements that tend to appeal to the different parts of the personality or temperament.[46]

5. Mistaken Attempts to Project Personality Types Onto Christ

In their desire to validate a personality indicator for use in the spiritual life the practitioners often like to project back personality types either on to our Lord himself or at least on to his apostles. It is suggested that each of the four gospels is (conveniently enough) written especially for one of the four main Jungian types so that taken together they reveal the Word of God for all to hear.[47] And Jesus is said to have all nine Enneagram types so that he can save people of all personalities.[48]

Clearly if our type is of central importance to our identity then we can't allow that Jesus is one type more than other types. For how could a 'J' save 'P's? Or an 'N' comprehend the reality of being an 'S'? He will either have to be a perfectly balanced individual on the boundaries of all types, or somehow contain all types within himself. But the point, of course, is that our personality is not that important. The key thing is that Christ is God become human; by taking our human nature upon himself God redeems humanity. Because Jesus was Jewish does not mean he can't save Gentiles; despite being single he still saves the married; despite being a carpenter he still saves the plumbers. Whatever personality type we like to imagine for Jesus is quite beside the point. Indeed once we start thinking in these terms our fascination with personality types has perhaps already gone further than is useful for promoting the spiritual life.

In conclusion, the church's growing interest in personality indicators sometimes merely reflects a secular culture where people are increasingly turning inwards to find resources to cope with life from within themselves. This can never be fully adequate for Christians. For we hold that wisdom and insight ultimately comes not from within our natural selves but from God (Eph 1.7). Moreover, an over-concern with self-analysis is sometimes obtained at the price of neglecting God and other people. Yet the church has always insisted that true self-knowledge is a necessary aspect of the spiritual life. And, as we have seen, personality indicators do promote self-knowledge and self-acceptance, as well as sensitizing us to variety and difference between people, and opening up for us alternative methods of prayer. To the extent that personality indicators lead us to a greater and more truthful awareness of ourselves as the wonderful but flawed creatures of our heavenly Creator they are to be valued. Augustine's prayer 'may I know myself; may I know thee' is still a valuable touchstone for the spiritual life. Where personality indicators are misconceived let us not be afraid to say so; where they are helpful let us not be afraid to use them.

46 So Michael and Norrisey, p 103ff.
47 Duncan, ch 5.
48 Beesing *et al*, p 49.